Careers Work IN SCHOOLS

A Primer for Career Development Facilitators

Catherine Hughes

AUSTRALIANACADEMIC**PRESS**

First published 2017 by:
Australian Academic Press Group Pty. Ltd.
18 Victor Russell Drive
Samford Valley QLD 4520, Australia
www.australianacademicpress.com.au

Careers Work in Schools: A Primer for Career Development Facilitators

ISBN   9781922117953 (paperback)
ISBN   9781922117960 (ebook)

Publisher: Stephen May
Copy editing: Rhonda McPherson
Cover design: Luke Harris, Working Type Studio
Typesetting: Australian Academic Press
Printing: Lightning Source

Contents

Acknowledgements

In my work as a school career practitioner I apply career development theory and research to career programs and interventions that address the career development needs of students and answer their career questions. I am therefore honoured that Professor Wendy Patton, a leading academic in the career development field and Carole Brown, a leading Australian career practitioner and Past President of the Career Development Association of Australia, kindly offered to review an earlier version of this book. I sincerely thank Wendy and Carole for their feedback and support in the writing of this book. The amendments made in response to their feedback make this book a more useful guide for career development facilitators who work with students from the upper middle years to the end of their secondary education.

About the Author

Catherine Hughes is the founder of the Grow Careers website, a self-help career information resource that applies lifelong career development in the context of a school, with intended audiences of students, parents or guardians, past students and school staff. She is currently a career counsellor at a school where she is responsible for career development programs and interventions for students from Years 7 to 12.

Catherine has achieved a PhD in vocational psychology, which included a study of adolescent career maturity and selected antecedents of career maturity across Australian and Thai cultural contexts. She has worked as a career practitioner in a variety of settings, including vocational rehabilitation, outplacement, private practice and has 30 years experience in designing and delivering career services in schools. Catherine has worked on national projects including being a member of the national writing teams for the *Australian Curriculum: Work Studies, Years 9 to 10* and for the Teacher Support Guide for this subject, delivering labour-market information workshops on behalf of the Career Development Association of Australia and contributing to the development of training materials for an early version of Australia's national career information and career exploration service.

Catherine has presented her work and research at national and international conferences. She has received national awards for her careers work in schools and her academic research.in the career developemtn field.

Connect with Dr Catherine Hughes

Friend me on Facebook:
https://www.facbook.com/Grow-Careers-878888328858924/timeline/

Follow me on Twitter:
https://twitter.com/Grow_Careers

Connect on LinkedIn:
https://www.linkedin.com/pub/catherine-hughes/30/114/262

Visit my website: http://www.growcareers.com.au

Preface

This book is one of a series of 'careers work in schools' books written to support the work of career development facilitators in schools, from those charged with teaching a work-related subject for the first time to seasoned school-based career practitioners wanting to refresh their knowledge, understanding and practice. The series is the culmination of my careers work in schools and my efforts develop expertise in adolescent career development and implement best practice in the design and delivery of career services.

Like so many career practitioners, my entry into careers work in schools was not planned and at the time I had no career development qualifications. Soon afterwards I enrolled in my first post-graduate qualification in career education. The immense value of career development qualifications for designing and delivering best-practice evidence-based career services in schools was clear. One thing led to another and I graduated with a Doctor of Philosophy in vocational psychology in 2012, involving a cross-cultural study of adolescent career development across Australian and Thai cultural contexts.

The content of Careers Work in Schools: A Primer for Career Development Facilitators is drawn from my now extensive practical experience in designing and delivering school-based career services, my understanding of theories of career development gained through my postgraduate study and research and my ongoing reading of the professional literature and research. The book starts with careers practice in schools. It begins with the career questions that school students in the middle and secondary years typically ask and the concerns of career development facilitators with responsibility for designing, delivering and evaluating career services in schools. How theories of career development answer the typical questions of middle and secondary school students and the concerns of career development facilitators is explained and further supported with evidence of the practical application of career theories in the form of tools and techniques to support careers work in schools.

Catherine Hughes, PhD

Chapter 1

The Context of Careers Work in Schools

Career development refers to the lifelong process of managing life, learning and work (Ministerial Council for Education, Early Childhood Development and Youth Affairs [MCEECDYA], 2010). An individual's career development can be influenced by a myriad of factors, from individual factors such as genetic predispositions, interests and skills, to social influences such as experiences in school, the family, the community, the friendship group, media and the workplace, to societal-environmental factors such as cultural, economic, geographic and political environments (Patton & McMahon, 2014). Schools, particularly in the secondary years, have been one of the main providers of services to support the career development of young people. School-based career development programs and services help young people develop attitudes, skills and knowledge to prepare for and adapt to multiple learning and work transitions throughout life (Savickas, 2011). This book aims to support those who plan and deliver career development programs for students in the upper middle and secondary school years.

Typically students in the middle and secondary school years make a series of choices with career implications such as curriculum choices (e.g., vocational education and training, academic), elective subject choices, volunteering, decisions about part-time work while at school or holiday jobs and decisions about post-school study options and initial occupation preferences. Towards the end of the secondary years, students take steps to implement these choices by applying for university, college or vocational education and training courses, applying for apprenticeships, and so on. The readiness of secondary school students to make and implement career decisions such as these can vary greatly and many students find the expectation to make and implement choices such as these confusing and sometimes stressful.

A variety of career development interventions support students to prepare for, make, and implement these career choices. Examples include career education classes, work-related courses, work-exposure activities, workshops, individual and group career counselling, computer-assisted career guidance, career information, and career assessments and their interpretation in individual or group settings. For the purpose of this book, these programs and career development interventions are collectively referred to as career services.

Who Does Careers Work in Schools?

A variety of members of school staff facilitate the career development of students. For some, careers work is central to their role within the school. For others, careers work may not be core work, but nevertheless these members of staff engage in activities intended to facilitate student career development. Examples of school staff who may engage in careers work in schools include:

1. Career practitioners who design, deliver and evaluate career services.

2. Teachers who integrate career development content into subject teaching, deliver a career development course or work-related subject, advise students about curriculum and subject choices, or incorporate activi-

ties designed to help students with career choices as part of their pastoral care role.

3. Student counsellors, pastoral care coordinators, chaplains and similar school staff who engage in careers work when they support and advise students with varying personal, social and academic concerns.

Following Patton and McMahon (2014), for the purposes of this book, all school staff involved in careers work will be referred to as career development facilitators. Career development facilitators need the relevant skills and knowledge to respond to the typical career questions and concerns of students and as a basis for designing, delivering and evaluating career services that develop students' capacity to manage multiple career transitions throughout life.

Career Questions and Concerns of Students

Career development facilitators working with students in the upper middle and secondary years are likely to be approached by students with career questions that are mainly about post-school learning and work options, subject choices, implementing career and course preferences, financial support for post-school study, and what action to take when there is a career problem. Examples of typical student career questions are:

1. What can I do when I leave school?

2. What jobs or occupations would suit me?

3. How do I prepare for my career?

4. How can I get information about different career options?

5. What courses will give me the qualifications I need for the occupations that interest me?

6. What are the entry requirements for the courses I want to study after I leave school?

7. What elective school subjects should I study to gain entry into courses I want to study?

8. How do I make career decisions?

9. How do I apply for courses I can do when I finish school?

10. What can I do if something happens that makes it difficult for me to get into the course or occupation I want?

11. What are the costs of education and training after I finish school?

12. What financial support is available?

13. How do I get a job?

Career Development Facilitator Concerns

Just as students have career questions, career development facilitators have concerns about how to design, deliver, and evaluate career services. Examples of typical career development facilitator concerns are:

1. What knowledge, skills and understandings do I need to support student career development?

2. What resources and sources of information are available to help students make career decisions and implement plans for what they want to do when they leave school?

3. How can schools meet the career development needs of all students?

4. How can career services be evaluated?

These typical career questions of students and school career development facilitators are addressed with reference to theories of career choice and development.

Chapter 2 provides an overview of theories of career development that are useful for careers work in schools. The student career questions and career development facilitator concerns they address are discussed. Chapter 3 discusses the practical application of career theories and related career tools for delivering career services in the upper middle and secondary school years. Chapter 4 discusses evaluation of career services. Concluding comments and a summary are provided in the final chapter.

Chapter 2

Theories of Career Development

Theories of career development guide career development facilitators in the selection of career interventions, their content, and delivery. Each career theory focuses on a specific range of vocational behaviours and problems. The vocational problems addressed and the populations served are key criteria in determining the usefulness of a theory as a guide to practice (Richardson, Constantine, & Washburn, 2005; Savickas, 2002). An overview of career theories relevant to school students in the upper middle and secondary years is presented, including the career questions addressed by each theory and contemporary applications.

From its beginnings as a field of scientific inquiry early in the 20th century to the present time there have been two major transitions in the vocational psychology and career development literature. A third transition is now becoming a widely accepted as a model of practice (Richardson et al., 2005). The first transition reflects a change from a concern with getting a job to a concern with what occupation to choose among a number of alternatives. The second transition reflects a change from the point of occupational choice to a concern with how career evolves over the life course (Savickas, 2002) and associated processes (Savickas & Baker, 2005). The third transition is concerned with why people make the various work and life choices they do as they respond to multiple learning and work transitions throughout life in the context of an ever-changing world (Savickas et al., 2009; Hartung, 2013a; Vondracek, Ford, & Porfeli, 2014).

The First Transition:
From Getting a Job to Choosing an Occupation
Person–Environment Career Theories

Person–environment fit theories are mainly concerned with 'occupations and the type of people who fill them' (Savickas, 2002, p. 150). They focus on individual differences, the resemblance of individuals to the requirements of different occupations, and choosing a congruent occupation or course among a range of alternatives. Person–environment fit theories assume that each person can be characterised by a unique pattern of traits such as abilities, interests, values, and needs and that occupations and work environments can be described in terms of personal attributes associated with success. Predictions can be made about an individual's degree of satisfaction with an occupation, course or activity. Career development practice based on person–environment fit theories falls into the guidance paradigm whereby career development facilitators guide students '... by recognizing who they resemble and then advising them to explore occupations in which similar people work' (Savickas, 2013a, p. 650).

Person–environment fit theories help students to answer questions about identifying congruent occupations and exploring post-school options. From the perspective of career development facilitators, person–environment fit theories partially address the knowledge, skills, and understandings needed to support students in identifying and exploring post-school options they are likely to find satisfying.

Holland's Theory of Vocational
Personalities and Work Environments

Holland's (1959, 1997) theory of vocational personalities and work environments is a well known, widely accepted and widely researched person–environment fit career theory.

Influenced by the interaction of biological and environmental factors, Holland's theory assumes that individuals develop a preference for some activities and an aversion to others. These preferences develop into interests and later related competencies and values. In turn they lead to the development of a disposition or vocational personality type with characteristic traits, attitudes, behaviours, and skill sets (1997, p. 18). Vocational personality is assumed to be a composite of six vocational personality types, although most people are assumed to resemble one vocational personality type more closely than others. Briefly, these types are:

1. Realistic, reflecting a manual, practical or outdoor orientation.

2. Investigative, reflecting a preference for using science and mathematics to solve problems.

3. Artistic, reflecting an orientation towards creative expression.

4. Social, reflecting a preference for roles and activities that involve people contact.

5. Enterprising, reflecting an orientation towards managerial, leadership, and persuasive roles and activities.

6. Conventional, reflecting an orientation towards conforming to established rules and procedures.

Six model environment types correspond to each of the six vocational personality types. The theory assumes that people prefer and seek out environments that match their vocational personality pattern, allowing them to use their talents and skills. An internet search will yield several credible sources of further information on Holland's (1959; 1997) theory.

Contemporary Applications of Person–Environment Fit Perspectives

Many career assessment instruments have been developed on the basis of the matching principles of person–environment fit theories. Career development interventions typically involve administering instruments to assess a person's unique set of traits at a point in time, and matching them to congruent work environments and courses of study. Many of these career assessment tools have been subjected to rigorous research, and are reliable and valid assessments of the personal characteristics they measure in cultural contexts similar to those in which the assessment instrument was developed, or for which it has been appropriately adapted. These career assessments are usually commercially available from publishers of psychological tests. Some career assessment tools based on person–environment fit principles are freely available on the internet. Some have undergone research and have adequate reliability and validity. However, the reliability and validity of some freely available career assessment tools is often not made clear and should be used with caution.

The Second Transition: From Point of Choice to Life-Span Career Development

Person–environment fit models in isolation are inadequate. Super (1983) argued that matching models make the unwarranted assumption that all people who are assessed have mature and stable traits and are ready and willing to use the self-knowledge provided by person–environment fit career assessments. Such matching models do not explain processes associated with career development over the life course, including how students become ready to make career choices and willing to use the knowledge gained from matching approaches.

Developmental career theories explain how an individual's career evolves and develops from infancy to post-retirement (Savickas, 2002) and processes associated with life-span career development (Richardson, 1993). Career practice based on developmental career theories falls into the career education paradigm whereby career practitioners 'help individuals develop the attitudes, beliefs, and competencies that they need to make viable career choices and realistic work adjustments' (Savickas, 2013a, p. 652).

For school students, the main question that developmental career theories address is 'How do I prepare for my career?'. In turn, this question guides students to seek answers to other typical career questions concerned with exploring self, the world of work, occupations and education and training options and their entry requirements, job and course application procedures, and making and implementing career decisions. From the perspective of career development facilitators, developmental career theories address the knowledge, skills and understandings that career development facilitators need to support students in managing their career throughout life as well as providing guidance in relation to the content of career interventions.

Developmental career theories either focus on career development across the whole of the life-span, or on a segment of the life-span. Life-span, life-space theory (Super, 1953, 1990), theory of circumscription and compromise (Gottfredson, 1981, 2005) and career construction theory (Savickas, 2002, 2013b) are developmental career theories, although career construction theory extends life-span, life-space career theory by incorporating a constructivist perspective.

Life-Span, Life-Space Theory

Life-span, life-space theory of career development supplements person–environment fit perspectives with a longitudinal view of careers (Super, 1990). Life-span, life-space, and self-concept are the three segments of the theory. Life-span focuses on stages of career development and the processes and developmental tasks associated with adapting to learning and work transitions throughout life (Super, Savickas, & Super, 1996; Hartung, 2013b). Five stages of life-span career development are Growth, Exploration, Establishment, Maintenance, and Decline (Super 1953, 1990). At each stage, individuals encounter vocational development tasks, or social expectations '… about preparing for, engaging in and reflecting upon a productive work life' (Super et al., 1996, p. 131).

At approximately 14 years of age, the Growth stage of career development gives way to the Exploration stage. Vocational development tasks of the Growth stage are concerned with developing a future orientation, a sense of control over one's life and the capacity to make decisions, confidence in one's abilities and acquiring competent work habits. During the exploration stage, individuals crystallise their vocational self-concept by developing awareness of their interests, abilities, and values, and the relationship of these to work and learning options. They build career decision-making skills, specify a preferred career direction and related educational pathways and make flexible plans and take steps to implement their career preferences (Super, Savickas, & Super, 1996).

Career maturity is an important concept derived from the life-span segment of life-span, life-space career theory. It is concerned with how well adolescents cope with the vocational development tasks of crystallising, specifying and implementing an initial career choice. Students with positive attitudes towards planning for, and exploring future vocational and educational choices as well as current knowledge about the world of work, occupations and related learning pathways and career decision-making confidence are more likely to success-fully deal with the vocational development tasks of the exploration stage (Super, 1983).

Life-space focuses on the social context in which career development occurs. It explains the interaction of various life roles and personal and situational factors that impact on career decisions (Super, 1980). Throughout life people move in and out of various life roles such as being a child, student, friend, worker, partner or spouse, parent, homemaker, retiree and person involved in leisure, hobby, community, spiritual or religious activities. Life roles fluctuate in impor-tance at different times in life. Secondary students who are more concerned about and committed to the work role tend to be more career mature (Lokan, 1992; Lokan & Shears, 1995; Patton & Creed, 2002).

For many school students in the middle and secondary years, life roles associated with family, friends, school, com-munity, and spiritual or religious activities tend to dominate their life. As students approach decision points such as choosing elective school subjects, choosing a curriculum type or making decisions about their next step after leaving school, the work role may not be important for some, leading to the possibility of poor choices that may limit future options.

The self-concept segment of life-span, life-space theory focuses on the content of career choice. In the context of life-span, life-space career theory, self-concept refers to vocational self-concept. Super (1953, 1990) proposed that people seek to express their vocational self-concept in work and work satisfac-tion is related to the degree to which vocational self-concept has been implemented at work (Super et al., 1996).

Theory of Circumscription and Compromise

Linda Gottfredson's (1981, 1996, 2002, 2005) theory of circumscription and compromise is concerned with career development in childhood and adolescence. The theory proposes that young people distinguish between occupations on the basis of sex type, prestige level and field of work. Circumscription refers to a process by which young people progressively eliminate occupations they regard as unacceptable on the basis of sex type, prestige level and ability level. Compromise refers to the process by which young people adjust their occupational preferences for more accessible and realistic, although potentially less compatible alternatives.

According to the theory, children as young as 6 to 8 years of age start to reject occupations that are perceived to be incompatible with their gender identity and by early adolescence young people are aware of an occupational hierarchy, have learned the types of occupations their families and communities reject on the basis of social prestige, and are aware of their intellectual ability relative to that of their peers (Gottfredson, 1981, 2002, 2005). These processes result in a zone of acceptable occupational alternatives, excluding occupations perceived to be of the wrong sex type, occupations perceived to be academically too demanding and occupations inconsistent with perceived social standing. This means that without intervention, many students may be unwilling to explore nontraditional career and course options.

Cognitive Information Processing Career Theory

There are many career theories that deal with processes associated with life-span career development (Savickas & Baker, 2005). Cognitive information processing career theory is one of these. Cognitive information processing theory is concerned with the knowledge base required for effective career problem-solving and decision-making, information process-ing skills that facilitate the transformation of self-knowledge and knowledge about learning and work options and the world of work into meaningful and satisfying career decisions throughout life (Peterson, Sampson, Lenz, & Reardon, 2002; Sampson, Lenz, Reardon, & Peterson, 1999). Cognitive infor-mation processing career theory has turned its attention to practical issues such as how to deliver cost-effective career services in contexts such as schools where the number of students to serve is large compared to the number of full-time equivalent career development facilitators (Sampson, Reardon, Peterson, & Lenz, 2004).

From the perspective of students, the main question that cognitive information processing career theory addresses is 'How do I make career decisions?'. From the perspective of school career development facilitators, cognitive information processing career theory addresses questions concerned with the knowledge, skills and understandings needed to support students in solving career problems, cost-effective career development services, and how to meet the career develop-ment needs of all students.

Cognitive information processing theory is represented as a pyramid of information processing domains pertinent to career problem-solving and decision-making and a problem solving and decision-making model that explains how infor-mation is processed to transform self and options knowledge into satisfying career choices throughout life (see Figure 2.1).

Self-knowledge includes interests, values, skills and abilities as well as other considerations such as personal circum-stances, social and environmental context and lifestyle preferences. Knowledge of options includes factual informa-tion about industries, occupations and how they are organised, specialisations, labour market conditions, different ways of working, education and training institutions, courses and associated costs. The decision-making domain includes

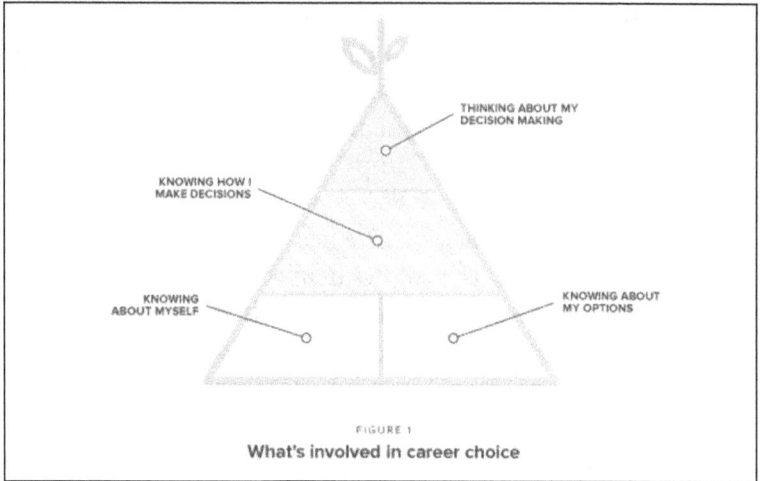

FIGURE 1
What's involved in career choice

Figure 2.1

The pyramid of information processing domains pertinent to career problem-solving and decision-making and a problem solving and decision-making model.
Source: 'A Cognitive Approach to Career Development and Services: Translating Concepts into Practice' by J.P. Sampson, Jr., G.W. Peterson, J.G. Lenz, and R.C. Reardon, 1992, The Career Development Quarterly, 41, p. 70. (Copyright 1992 by the National Career Development Association. All rights reserved. Reprinted with permission.)

knowing how to make important decisions. The executive processing domain includes metacognitions associated with reflecting on the decision-making process and progress, being aware of and managing thoughts during the process, maintaining motivation to get all the needed information and knowing when enough information has been obtained to make an informed decision.

The decision-making skills domain is comprised of generic information processing skills that people use to solve problems. Cognitive information processing career theory refers to this process as the CASVE cycle (see Figure 2.2).

The information processing elements of the CASVE cycle are:

1. Communication from external or internal cues of a career problem or gap between current situation and a

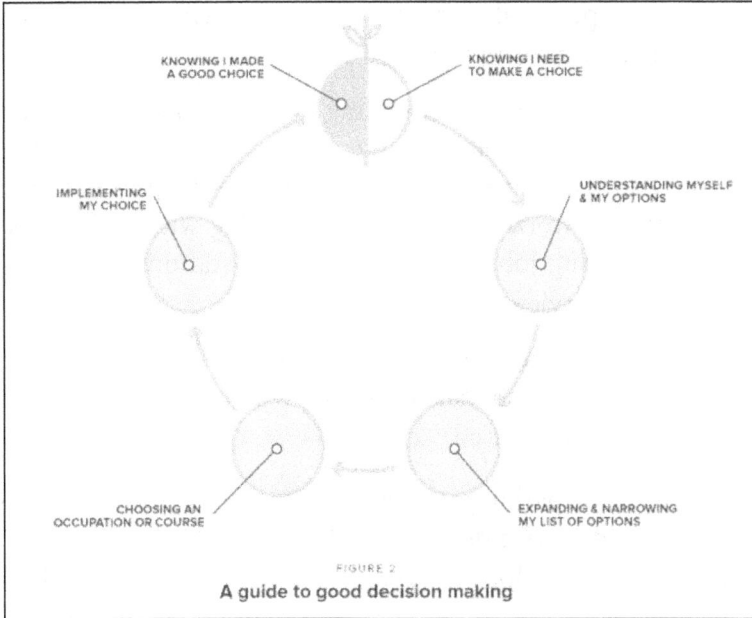

FIGURE 2
A guide to good decision making

Figure 2.2

CASVE cycle.

Source: 'A Cognitive Approach to Career Development and Services: Translating Concepts into Practice,' by J.P. Sampson, Jr., G.W. Peterson, J.G. Lenz, and R.C. Reardon, 1992, The Career Development Quarterly, 41, p. 70. (Copyright 1992 by the National Career Development Association. All rights reserved. Reprinted with permission.)

desired situation (e.g., having to choose school subjects for the following year).

2. Analysis of self and options knowledge.

3. Synthesis, involving expanding the range of options being considered based on interests, values, skills and abilities, and then narrowing the options to a manageable list.

4. Valuing, involving making an optimal tentative choice after comparing the top 3 to 5 alternatives. This may include consideration of factors such as family situa-

tion, personal circumstances, life preferences, labour market information, and so on.

5. Execution, or implementing a choice. This may include actions such as making a flexible plan to get the required education and training, attending career fairs, getting work experience, networking with employers, preparing job application documentation, rehearsing job interview skills, and more.

6. Using metacognitive strategies to monitor whether the career problem has been dealt with or whether further action is required.

Cognitive information processing career theory recommends a differentiated service delivery model where students are allocated to self-help, brief-staff assisted or individual case-managed levels of career service delivery on the basis of readiness screening. The self-help level of service provides minimal career development facilitator input. Students independently use career resources, but are able to seek the support of a career development facilitator if needed. Brief-staff assisted services involve career development facilitators supporting students in a group setting such as a workshop or career education class. Individual case-managed services are provided to students with the greatest need as determined by readiness screening.

Contemporary Applications of Developmental and Process Career Theories

The emergence of developmental career theories led to the implementation of career education as a career intervention. The aim of career education is to orient individuals to the vocational development tasks they will encounter and prepare them to manage these tasks by developing self-regulatory attitudes, behaviours and competencies that will enable them to successfully cope with vocational development tasks throughout life (Savicaks, 2013a).

Career development frameworks that identify lifelong career management competencies, such as the Australian Blueprint for Career Development, the Canadian Blueprint for Life, England's Blueprint for Careers, the Career Management Skills Framework for Scotland, and the US National Career Development Guidelines are examples of the contemporary application of developmental career theories.

The content of a number of career exploration websites reflects a developmental perspective. For example, Australia's myfuture website mainly provides resources to assist individuals to negotiate the crystallisation, specification and implementation vocational development tasks associated with the Exploration stage of career development.

Career assessment instruments have been developed to assess constructs from life-span, life-space theory, career construction theory and cognitive information processing career theory perspectives. Measures of career maturity were developed soon after the emergence of life-span, life-space theory. However, career construction theory's refinement of life-span, life-space theory (Savickas, 2002) has updated the concept of 'career maturity' to 'career adaptability'. Measures of career maturity or career adaptability can be used to assess how well students are managing vocational development tasks, as a basis for developing career interventions, as a pre- and post-test assessment to evaluate the effectiveness of career interventions or as a readiness screening instrument to allocate students to an initial level of career service delivery in accordance with a cognitive information processing career theory approach.

Cognitive information processing career theory gives career information more prominence than some other theoretical perspectives, with knowledge of options being one of the domains for effective career problem-solving and decision-making. Career information is conveyed through a variety of digital, print, audiovisual and people resources and experiential activities. The need for career practitioners and career development facilitators to have a sound and up-to-date knowledge of career information and its various sources and to store these in a physical and/or virtual library is arguably one of the main features of that distinguishes career counselling from other counselling work.

The Third Transition: Subjective Career

Responding to Pepper's (1942) proposition that contextualism is one of four world views, each with a different perspective on the construal of reality, a number of authors have drawn attention to careers work from the perspective of the contextualist world view. Contextualism regards individuals and their context as a whole, inseparable and interpenetrating; a person-in-context unit (Richardson et al., 2005; Young, Valach, & Collin, 2002). Careers work that seeks to understand the reality of a person-in-context unit is practised from a constructivist epistemological perspective. Constructivism is directly derived from contextualism (Patton & McMahon, 1999). By applying constructivist techniques, career development facilitators seek to understand the subjective reality of career as constructed and lived by human beings in the context of their everyday lives (Blustein, 2006; Hartung, 2015; Richardson, 1993; Richardson et al., 2005; Savickas, 1993; 2011). Professional practice based on constructivism falls into the career construction counselling or life designing paradigm (Savickas, 2013a; Savickas et al., 2009). This counselling model engages students in telling their career story, reflecting on its themes and projecting these into the future.

Career construction theory (Savickas, 2002, 2005, 2013b), systems theory framework (Patton & McMahon, 1999, 2006, 2014) and chaos theory of careers (Pryor & Bright, 2011) are three theoretical perspectives that reflect this approach to career development and practice. Aspects of these three theoretical perspectives that are salient to careers work in schools are discussed next.

Career Construction Theory

Career construction theory is a refined, updated and expanded version of Super's (1990) life-span, life-space theory (Savickas, 2002). Career construction theory responds to the needs of individuals in a global economy, characterised by change, uncertainty, fragmented career pathways, and an imperative for individuals to adapt to multiple transitions across variety of work assignments or jobs over the course of their lives (Savickas et al., 2009). It retains aspects of matching and earlier developmental perspectives that are useful in a changing world of work and enhances these with counselling interventions that help individuals to reflect on their life themes and the meaning of these for constructing their career (Savickas, 2013a).

Career development facilitators can apply career construction theory to enable students to find answers to most typical student career questions. Student questions about preparing for their future career can be addressed through the development of career adaptability attitudes, beliefs and competencies. Career decision-making questions can be explored through life themes and stories of previous career decision-making confidence and success. For career development facilitators career construction theory addresses questions about the knowledge, skills and understandings needed to support student career development.

Career construction theory defines career as '… a reflection on the course of one's vocational behavior …' (Savickas, 2002, p. 152). For school students in the middle and secondary years such reflection may focus on objective career; that is, actual events such as part-time, casual or holiday jobs held, school subject choices, sports participation, hobbies, community service activities, volunteer work, chores around the home, and so on.

Career adaptability denotes career choice readiness and self-regulatory strengths that individuals can draw on to solve career problems and cope with the demands of vocational development tasks, work traumas and career transitions (Savickas, 2002, 2012). These self-regulatory resources are attitudes, beliefs and competencies associated with concern about one's vocational future, a belief that one has some personal control over it by exploring, refining and deciding, attitudes of curiosity expressed by exploring self and possible future learning and work scenarios, and confidence in taking steps to pursue one's aspirations (Savickas, 2013b).

Life themes reveal the meaning underlying the unique and diverse ways that individuals fit work into their lives and construct their career throughout life. Life themes explain why individuals do what they do; why they make the work-related choices they make. Through interventions such as life designing counselling (Savickas, 2012, 2015) students are encouraged to extend life themes into possible selves and future work scenarios (Savickas, 2013b).

Systems Theory Framework of Career Development

Factors that influence career development have been positioned within a systems theory structure to form a map of all influences on an individual's career development (Patton & McMahon, 1999, 2006, 2014). A unique aspect of systems theory framework is its application to the career counselling process and the therapeutic system that arises when the career development facilitator and student meet for career counselling (Patton & McMahon, 1999, 2006, 2014).

As systems theory framework of career development recognises the contribution of all career theories (Patton & McMahon, 1999, 2006, 2014), it indirectly addresses all the typical career questions of students in the middle and secondary years. For school career development facilitators, systems theory framework responds to questions about the knowledge, skills and understandings needed to support student career development and the most appropriate system (individual, social or societal/environmental) from which to intervene to bring about improved career development outcomes. In addition, systems theory framework promotes reflective practice by encouraging career development facilitators to reflect on the quality of the career counselling relationship and by considering their own career development, its influences and how these might interact with student career development.

Systems theory framework is depicted as concentric circles representing the individual system, the social system and the societal/environmental system. A range of subsystems that represent influences on career development populate each system. Influences in the individual system include interests, abilities, skills, aptitudes, values, beliefs, self-concept, personality, sexual orientation, health status, disability, world of work knowledge, age, gender, and ethnicity. The social system reflects the social context in which an individual's career development occurs, and includes the subsystems of family, education institutions, peers, the workplace, community groups, and the media. The societal/environment system includes the subsystems of socioeconomic status, the employment market, geographic location, globalisation, historical trends, and political decisions. The systems and subsystems of systems theory framework are open to influence from other systems and subsystems, which can be nonlinear, acausal, multidirectional, or mutual. Change over time and chance, or unplanned occurrences can influence any part of a system, and in turn an individual's career development. The systems theory framework of career development uses the construct of story to identify and understand patterns and relationships between systems and subsystems of influence on the career development of an individual.

As systems theory framework of career development acknowledges all other career theories and highlights interrelationships between them, it can serve as a guide for career development facilitators wishing to incorporate other theories into their practice while adhering to a systems theory perspective. For example, a career development facilitator may include Holland's (1997) typology of work personalities and environments to help a student understand the relationship between interests (individual system) and work environments (social system). Similarly, a career development facilitator may draw upon Gottfredson's (2002) theory of circumscription and compromise to explore the influence of the gender (individual system) and socioeconomic status (societal/environmental system) on the student's career development.

Chaos Theory of Careers

Several theoretical approaches to career development acknowledge that an individual's career development is complex and influenced by change, chance and unplanned events. However, only recently Pryor and Bright (2003) applied chaos theory to career development. Pryor and Bright (2003; 2011) explain that their chaos theory of careers is the only sound theoretical account of career development realities of the interplay of structure and development, stability and non-linear change, predictability and chance, complexity and limitations of knowledge (Pryor, Amundson, & Bright, 2008; Pryor & Bright, 2015) that individuals negotiate as they construct their career over the life course.

Chaos theory of careers responds to typical student career questions about post-school options and preparing for one's career. Specifically, it encourages students to keep an open mind about post-school options and career possibilities and to be open to new opportunities. For career development facilitators, chaos theory of careers responds to the knowledge, skills and understandings needed to support student career development.

The chaos theory of careers' concern with order and stability as well as change and chance (Bright & Pryor, 2008) is important for school career development facilitators. There is much order and stability in school contexts. Every year students make decisions about school subjects they will study in the following year, every year students have the opportunity to undertake a range of co-curricular or extracurricular activities, and in some schools students in one or more year groups are required to complete a learning or transition plan. Change and chance are also common. In an unpredictable world, students make subject choices and some may develop learning or transitions plans with limited knowledge about the full range of possibilities for their future work life. On this basis, chaos theory of careers encourages students to develop ongoing flexible plans for their future so that they can respond to likely chance, change and unpredictability. It encourages schools to provide the support structures for students to develop, modify or redevelop flexible learning, work and transition plans (Bright & Pryor, 2008).

Contemporary Applications of Constructivist Career Theories

Constructivist career theories have stimulated the development of qualitative career assessment methods and tools to add to the toolkit of career development facilitators. Life designing and narrative methods of career counselling assist individuals to clarify their identity and life themes and the meaning of these for shaping and managing their career in the context of their unique life-space and the society in which they live. My Career Story (Savickas & Hartung, 2012) and My System of Career Influences (McMahon, Patton, & Watson, 2005), are just two of the growing number of qualitative career assessment tools to support career development facilitators in applying constructivist and life design approaches to their practice. Constructivist career perspectives support the use of quantitative assessments when appropriate (Savickas, 2012).

Career development theories guide the planning, delivery and evaluation of school career services. The next chapter discusses the application of career development theory to careers work in schools.

Chapter 3

Applying Career Theory to Careers Work in Schools

Schools vary in the scope and nature of career development services they provide. Some schools offer an extensive range of career development services, while others offer a more restricted range. Schools also vary in the ratio of career development facilitators to students, career development facilitator qualifications, support for professional development of career development facilitators, and the financial and physical resources available for career services. Regardless of school context, best-practice means that school career development services should be soundly underpinned by career development theory. This chapter outlines how career development theories can be applied to school career services for students in the upper middle years through to the end of secondary education; that is, from Years 7 to 12.

Applying Developmental Career Theories

First and foremost, career services for students in the upper middle and secondary years should be guided by developmental career theories. A comprehensive career education program over all or at least several school years is important. Career interventions should be consistent with students' stage of career development and should enhance student career adaptability and their capacity to successfully negotiate the vocational development tasks they encounter.

Content Related to Vocational Development Tasks

To assist students to formulate their career preferences, career interventions in the upper middle years should facilitate students' awareness of their self-concept, career interests, abilities, and values as a basis for broad-based career exploration. In the secondary years career interventions need to develop students' capacity to narrow down career possibilities to a more manageable list for in-depth exploration so that they can make decisions about their initial career preferences and develop flexible plans to implement these preferences. Career exploration in the secondary years might focus on occupation and course options and their requirements, the world of work and its unpredictable and changing nature, new ways of working, emerging opportunities, work creation opportunities, making sense of labour market information, meeting the entry requirements for post-school education and training, job seeking and job keeping skills, and related documentation and strategies to maintain employability throughout life.

Content Related to Work Role Salience

For many students in the upper middle and early secondary years, the work role may seem remote. They may be preoccupied with activities associated with being a family member, a student, a friend, or a person involved in hobbies, recreational pursuits, community or spiritual activities. Career interventions to develop students' awareness of the choices that they make at school that can have an influence on the educational and career options open to them in their post-school years and a concern for future work roles may be required.

Content Related to Career Adaptability

In a changing world of work it is important that career interventions explicitly set out to develop the attitudes, behaviours, competencies and self-regulatory capacities that will enable students to self-manage multiple learning and work transitions throughout life. Thus, career interventions should set out to develop and monitor students' concern for their work futures, their capacity to exercise control and make informed decisions in relation to their learning and work future, their curiosity about possible learning and work scenarios and the self-confidence to implement their preferences.

Tools to Support Developmental Career Programs

1. Career Development Frameworks

The frameworks for career development in various countries enable schools to map existing career development provision, identify gaps in career services, design and match resources to career competencies and plan and deliver comprehensive and developmentally appropriate career services that build students' capacity to self-manage their career throughout life and to adapt to a changing and unpredictable world of work. A range of accompanying resources and tools support career development facilitators with responsibility for designing, implementing and evaluating career development services. The Australian Blueprint for Career Development is a helpful example.

The Australian Blueprint for Career Development comprises 11 career competencies and a range of resources for planning, developing, implementing and evaluating career development programs, interventions, products and support materials. The 11 career competencies are broad learning goals for career development that have been identified as essential for individuals to manage life, learning and work in a continually changing world. The career competencies span three areas of career development learning, and four developmental phases, from childhood through to adulthood. The three areas of career development in the Australian framework are personal management, learning and work exploration and career building.

1. Personal management career competencies are:

    - Build and maintain a positive self-image.
    - Interact positively and effectively with others.
    - Change and grow throughout life.

2. Learning and work exploration career competencies are:

    - Participate in lifelong learning supportive of career goals.
    - Locate and effectively use career information.
    - Understand the relationship between work, society and the economy.

3. Career building career competencies are:

    - Secure/create and maintain work.
    - Make career enhancing decisions.
    - Maintain balanced life and work roles.
    - Understand the changing nature of life and work roles.
    - Understand, engage in and manage the career building process.

The four developmental phases reflect career development across the life-span. While the appropriate developmental phase is intended to be determined on the basis of career development needs, in a school context the developmental phases of the Australian Blueprint for Career Development can be viewed as age based. The Australian developmental phases are:

- Phase I – pre-school/kindergarten to primary

- Phase II – middle years

- Phase III – senior/post-compulsory years

- Phase IV – adults.

Each of the 11 career competencies has a set of performance indicators across four learning stages. Performance indicators are specific learning objectives that describe the knowledge, skills, and attitudes that are needed to master the career competencies. The performance indicators form the basis for planning career development learning experiences and interventions and for and establishing local standards that specify what learners are required to do, under what conditions and how well in order to achieve competency.

The resources that accompany the Australian Blueprint for Career Development help career development facilitators: (a) determine the career development needs of students, and the career development competencies to priortise in career development programs and interventions; (b) record career development activities in terms of the competencies covered; (c) assess student of level of mastery of each of the career competencies; and (d) code career development products and resources. Case studies that illustrate the implementation of the Australian Blueprint for Career Development in a variety of settings provide additional support for career development facilitators.

2. Career Adaptability

The Career Adapt-Abilities Scale (Savickas & Porfeli, 2012) can be used to assess how well students are likely to manage vocational development tasks. This instrument assesses career adaptability strengths of concern, control, curiosity and confidence. It can also be used as a basis for developing career interventions to strengthen career adaptability and to measure of the outcomes of career interventions that aim to improve career adaptability. The instrument can be administered to a class or year cohort prior to the commencement of a career education intervention and again at its conclusion. Analysis of the pre-test administration would reveal career adaptability strengths among the student group as well as highlighting career adaptability attitudes, behaviours and competencies that may need to be strengthened. Post-test results can be used to evaluate the effectiveness of the career interventions and to promote the benefits of school career services to the school community. The international version of Career Adapt-Abilities Scale can be accessed via the *Journal of Vocational Behavior* (Savickas & Porfeli, 2012) or www.vocopher.com. Over a period of time, schools can develop their own local norms for each of the scales and for the whole instrument.

Career development facilitators who do not feel confident with the career adaptability construct and the Career Adapt-Abilities Scale (Savickas & Porfeli, 2012) may consider using a checklist of career development competencies, such as those available in an appendix of the Australian Blueprint for Career Development. Students could complete the checklist prior to a career intervention. Once the career intervention has been completed students could complete the checklist again for an indication of the influence of the intervention on career development.

3. Work Role Salience

One useful tool is the series of three animations on Australia's myfuture website, called 'the adventures of you'. These animations are intended to help students to develop their executive function. However, the animations take a life–career focus and encourage students to stop and think about the choices they are making. These animations may be used as a stimulus for students to reflect on the importance of work role and how many of the choices they make at school such as subject choices, co-curricular or extracurricular choices or how much effort to put into school subjects can have an impact on the range of course and career options open to them in their early post-school career.

Person–Environment Fit Theories

As previously discussed, a common career intervention from a person–environment fit perspective involves administering career tests to assess student individual factors such as vocational personality profile, career interest preferences, career value preferences and skills at a particular point in time and matching that information to currently congruent occupations. Mostly students enjoy activities of this nature. Often such instruments support students' view of how they see themselves and this may give students greater confidence in the potential suitability of occupations suggested by the results. The diversity of compatible occupations suggested by the results often surprises students and may expand the range of alternatives they explore further.

For students who have not previously given a lot of thought to future work possibilities and related courses, person–environment fit instruments are a useful stimulus for career exploration (Sampson, 2009). Person–environment fit instruments can be administered to individual students, a class group, or even a year cohort. Students are usually able to finish a person–environment fit instrument and briefly review the results within a single lesson. In subsequent lessons students can begin their career exploration starting with some of the suggested occupations.

Using Person–Environment Fit Tools Developmentally

Person–environment fit career assessment instruments can be used in a developmental way. Career assessment tests can be administered to students on two or more occasions during their middle and secondary years; for example, in Year 8, Year 10 and Year 12. Indeed, this is important, as vocational personality, interest or work value preferences may not be stable in the middle years. Examination of profile stability and change over time may provide helpful information for students to assist them to make initial decisions about career preferences, related education and training courses and school subject choices in their senior secondary years.

Person–environment fit instruments generate many potentially suitable occupations. In the middle and early secondary years students should be encouraged to explore the suggested occupations and related occupations, including those that are nontraditional for their gender. Sometimes students are disappointed that an occupation they had been considering was not suggested by the person–environment fit assessment instrument. Encouraging students to reflect on the factors that influenced the choice of their preferred occupation and to gain detailed information about that occupation may help students to gain a better understanding of the matching principles of person–environment fit approaches and comprehensive knowledge about their preferred occupation. For example, a student with the top three vocational personality types of Conventional, Social and Realistic may wonder why their preferred occupation of lawyer was not suggested as a potentially congruent occupation. It may be revealed that the student's parents influenced the career preference of lawyer, and that a law degree can be combined with a range of other degree options, some of which are congruent with the top three vocational personality types.

Using Person–Environment Fit Tools from a Constructivist Perspective

As previously noted, constructivist career theories do not preclude the administration of person–environment fit instruments (McMahon & Watson, 2012, 2015; Pyror & Bright, 2015; Savickas, 2012; Watson & McMahon, 2014). Administration of a quantitative career assessment instrument such as the Self-Directed Search could be followed by completion of an activity based on the Integrated Structured Interview (ISI: McMahon & Watson, 2012; Watson & McMahon, 2014). The ISI involves students in crafting small career stories about their quantitative career assessment results. The ISI could form part of an individual interpretation and feedback session delivered in a one-to-one career counselling or group intervention (McMahon & Watson, 2012). There are six sections of the ISI intervention:

1. Crafting a story about the quantitative results and scores. Students are invited to express their personal explanation of the results. Prompt questions may ask students how the results relate to their self-concept and personal attributes.

2. Crafting a story about the relative value of the quantitative scores. Students are invited to locate their top three vocational personality categories on scale of 1 to 10 and explain their placement and relative distance from each other.

3. Crafting a story about the quantitative scores in different life contexts. This section integrates the quantitative results with the student's life context. Prompt questions ask students to consider how each of their top vocational personality categories are evident in various life role contexts such as family life, leisure and recreational pursuits, spiritual or religious engagement, activities they enjoy with their peers, and school life including subjects they enjoy and co-curricular or extracurricular activities they enjoy.

4. Crafting a story about the quantitative career assessment results in work contexts. This section encourages students to explore relationships between quantitative career assessment results and any past and present paid and unpaid work roles such casual employment, community service, volunteer work, or work within the family.

5. Crafting a story about the quantitative career assessment results through personal reflection. Students are invited to reflect on the career stories they have constructed in the ISI process and identify their personal qualities, strengths and weaknesses that emerge from these stories.

6. Crafting a future career story using the quantitative career assessment results and the meaning attributed to them through the previous stories. (Watson & McMahon, 2014, p. 635).

Using the Language of Person–Environment Fit Theories

Even if the career development facilitator chooses not to administer person–environment fit instruments, the typology of vocational personality and corresponding work environment types, career interest types, or work value categories give students a language to describe their vocational personality and to describe work environments in terms of the attributes of people who are likely to experience satisfaction and success. During the process of life-design counselling, students may reflect on their stories about the types of environments to which they are attracted and the types of people they like to be with by drawing on the language of relevant person–environment fit typologies. Further, an understanding of such typologies can help students to classify learning or work opportunities that come their way throughout life, to estimate how compatible they might be and to create compatible work opportunities.

Person–Environment Fit Tools

There are many reliable and valid person–environment fit instruments available in the marketplace. Some can only be purchased and administered by registered psychologists. Some can be purchased and administered by professionals who are deemed to have adequate training in understanding psychometric tests. Some career assessment instruments can only be purchased and administered by individuals who have successfully completed a training course related to the instrument. Schools wishing to administer person–environment fit assessment instruments may need to investigate the availability of cost-effective, culturally relevant, reliable and valid instruments that can be administered and interpreted by relevant members of school staff. The Self-Directed Search and the Strong Interest Inventory are two examples of reliable and valid career assessment instruments based on Holland's theory of vocational personalities and work environments.

Some career assessment tools based on person–environment fit principles are freely available on the internet. Some of these have undergone research and have been found to have adequate reliability and validity. However, the reliability and validity of many freely available career assessment tools is often not made clear and caution should be exercised if instruments of unknown reliability and validity are administered to students. Examples of freely available online career assessment tools based on person–environment fit theories that have undergone research to establish psychometric properties include the Career Interest Test (Athanasou, 2000, 2007; Bartlett, Perera, & McIlveen, 2015), which has been incorporated into Australia's career profile service on the myfuture website (Education Services Australia, 2015) and the O*Net Interest Profiler (Rounds et al., 1999) available on the US national career information website (US Department of Labor, 2015).

Constructivist Career Theories

A clear implication of constructivist career theories is that career interventions should incorporate qualitative career assessment methods. These qualitative career assessment methods encourage students to convey stories about past and present experiences that explain the context of their career development, life patterns and themes and their personal meaning for constructing and enacting future learning and work scenarios.

While one-to-one life design counselling is an ideal intervention for qualitative career assessment, this is not possible in all school contexts as there are simply too many students and too few career development facilitators. However, as previously noted, qualitative career interventions can be blended with person–environment fit and career education approaches to career service delivery (Sampson, 2009; Savicaks, 2012; Watson & McMahon, 2014). Career education classes or career development workshops may involve students in completing qualitative career assessment instruments to complement more traditional person–environment fit approaches.

Constructivist Tools

A recent text by McMahon and Watson (2015) has been devoted to qualitative career assessment. This book contains numerous examples of qualitative career assessment tools and their use in practice. The various qualitative tools are ordered by learning style. Visual learning style qualitative career assessment tools include genogram, card sort, lifeline and storyboard tools. Auditory learning style tools include career construction interview formats, early recollection techniques, My Career Chapter (McIlveen 2006; McIlveen, Ford, & Dun, 2005) and challenging limiting career assumptions. Career writing, and My System of Career Influences (McMahon, & Watson, 2015) are offered qualitative career assessment tools aligned with a kinesthetic learning style preference.

My Career Story (Savickas & Hartung, 2012) is freely available from www.vocopher.com. This tool can form part of a career education course or workshop as well as being used in small group or individual life-design career counselling.

In the middle years and even in the secondary years some students it may find it difficult to provide detailed responses to questions intended to help them construct their career story by recalling their thoughts and feelings about aspects of their lives and reflecting on the themes these stories reveal and their meaning for future career scenarios. Career development facilitators may need to identify or create concrete qualitative career assessment tools. The digital or traditional career collage activity described by Loader (2009), a personal or career portfolio and a lifeline activity where students identify significant aspects of their lives (Brott, 2001) are examples of concrete activities that can be used as reflective tools for exploring self, life themes, and projecting these into learning and work possibilities for the future.

Similar to person–environment fit tools, qualitative career assessments can be used in a developmental way. For example, students could complete their 'identity collage' in the middle years, store it electronically and complete another identity collage in their secondary years. Similarly, students could complete tools such as My System of Career Influences (McMahon, Patton & Watson, 2005), My Career Chapter (McIlveen 2006; McIlveen, Ford, & Dun, 2005) or My Career Story (Savickas & Hartung, 2012) and with career development facilitator support, review, modify, and reflect on the meaning of these for future career scenarios on a number of occasions during their secondary education. Regular reflection, review, and modification of career assessment activities is in harmony with the chaos career theory view that a shift from developing a 'career plan' to ongoing flexible career planning is needed in a world of work characterised by change, uncertainty, unpredictability and chance (Bright & Pryor, 2007).

Cognitive Information Processing Career Theory

Cognitive information processing career theory is useful for school career services. The theory teaches career problem-solving and career decision-making skills and the client versions of models that have been developed to explain the theory are easy to remember and are suitable for students in the middle and secondary years. Students need to be taught how to solve career problems and make career decisions to enhance their career adaptability so that they can make informed learning and work decisions while at school and throughout life. They also need easy access to up-to-date, accurate and relevant information to facilitate effective career problem-solving and decision-making during the school years and throughout life.

The information base, decision-making skills, metacognitive strategies and problem solving processes needed to solve career problems and make career decisions throughout life can be reinforced by presenting the client version of the Pyramid of Information Processing Domains and the CSAVE career problem-solving model to students regularly throughout the middle and secondary years and reviewing the application of these to current career concerns and future transitions. For example, these models could be reinforced when commencing a new career education unit or workshop, in introductory sessions of a career development seminars or expos, when preparing students for a work exposure activity, or in small group or individual career counselling.

Differentiated Career Service Delivery Model

Cognitive information processing career theory's differentiated model of career service delivery enables schools to implement the highly effective career intervention of one-to-one career counselling (Whiston, 2002) to students who are in most need of this service (Sampson, Reardon, Peterson, & Lenz, 2004). The Career Thoughts Inventory (Sampson et al., 1996) for senior secondary students, the Career Adapt-Abilities Scale (Savickas & Porfeli, 2012) or a career competency survey constructed from a lifelong career development framework such as the Australian Blueprint for Career Development could be used to identify those who need one-to-one support and those for whom group or self-help interventions may suffice in the immediate term. One-to-one life design career counselling may be provided for those with the greatest need and other career interventions such as group career counselling, workshops, or career education classes can be offered to students with high levels of readiness and low levels of career development need. The differentiated career service delivery model is cost-effective and time-efficient. It enables the career development needs of all students to be met and can simultaneously make time available for other career interventions; for example, interventions to improve career development outcomes of groups facing disadvantage such as indigenous populations, students with a disability, students at risk of exiting school early, or refugees and migrants (Hughes & Lenz, 2011). Indeed, the differentiated service approach supported by the cognitive information processing approach to careers is so useful in school settings that it is the subject of another book in the careers work in schools series.

Career Resource Library

The information base for effective career problem-solving and career decision-making draws attention to the need for schools to provide students with relevant, up-to-date and accurate career information that is relevant to their career development needs. Print, digital, and audiovisual career information resources need to be acquired, developed, classified and stored in a location where that they can be quickly and easily located, retrieved and used by students and career development facilitators. Career information is typically housed in a library-like facility, which may range from a small collection of career information resources in one part of a career centre to a multipurpose career information library with provision for career workshops, career class visits, career counselling, and self-directed use of career resources (Gollert, 2003).

Sampson and colleagues (2004) apply information management techniques used by professional librarians to the development of career resource libraries. These authors note that librarians are experts in developing systems to help people locate and retrieve information resources. Thus, consultation with the school librarian is a useful starting point for the creation of a school career information resource library or update of an existing collection. Ongoing collaboration between the career and library professionals is important for continuous improvement of the school career information resource library.

Sampson and colleagues (2004) identify a number of considerations that should be taken into account when developing a career resource library. Those that are relevant to schools are summarised.

Location of the Career Resource Library

Depending on the school context, career information resources may be located in a specialist career library in a school career centre, a subunit of the school library, or they may form part of the general collection of a school library. An advantage of a specialist career library in a career centre is that career information resources are located where careers work is done and can be quickly accessed as and when needed at the time that career development facilitators or career practitioners are working with students. An advantage of locating career information resources within a subunit of the school library or as part of the school library's general collection is that acquisition, cataloguing, storing, retrieval and borrowing functions would be supported by existing school library staff. Wherever career information resources are located, it is imperative that they can be easily accessed and quickly retrieved by students using them in a self-directed capacity and by career development facilitators when they are working with students.

Physical Layout Considerations

The career information library space should be planned to encourage self-directed information seeking behaviour on a drop-in basis. Shelves, display stands, carrels, computers, tables, chairs, couches or other comfortable seating appropriately placed with physical separation of shelving and furniture can assist in making the career information library a user-friendly space.

Classification of Career Information

Career information resources located in a general collection in a school library may be classified and catalogued using the school library's existing system. A specialist career information resource library that is a subunit of the school library or a library housed in a career centre may adopt an alternative and perhaps self-made classification system. In a school context, it may be appropriate to classify career information in terms of one of the career development competency frameworks. For example, in an Australian context, career information resources could be classified under the Australian Blueprint for Career Development domains of Personal Management, Learning and Work Exploration and Career Building. Such a system would have sufficient flexibility to incorporate new resources and information. However, fact sheets and guides may be beneficial to facilitate ease of access for self-help users of the career information resource library (Gollert, 2003).

The Canadian Career Information Association has developed a resource with guidelines for the development and maintenance of career information libraries. The fifth edition of the book (Gollert, 2003) can be downloaded from the internet. While technological change has rendered some of the suggested computer products as somewhat dated, the processes described in the book are helpful to career development facilitators with responsibility for creating or maintaining a small collection in a career centre to a multipurpose specialist career library.

Designing Career Interventions

When designing career services, programs and interventions it is useful to consider meta-analytic research that has evaluated the effectiveness of career interventions. Overall, meta-analytic research has shown that career interventions across the board are moderately effective, although there is variation in the effectiveness of different types of career interventions (Whiston, 2002; Whiston & Buck, 2008; Whiston, Sexton, & Lasoff, 1998).

Brown and Ryan Krane (2000) and Brown et al. (2003) described five ingredients critical to effective career interventions, regardless of the theoretical orientation or the intervention modality. The five critical ingredients of effective career interventions identified by their meta-anaytic research are:

1. Workbooks, written exercises and homework activities that engage students in recording career information, their career goals and flexible career plans and action steps to make progress towards achieving their career goals.

2. Opportunities for students to receive individual interpretation of career assessments and their career goals and plans.

3. Opportunities for students to gather information on the world of work and possible future career options.

4. Opportunities for students to connect with role models and mentors to support them with vocational development tasks such as career exploration, career decision-making, and implementing career and educational preferences.

5. Activities that help students to build support networks to assist with their career choices and plans.

Designing and implementing theoretically sound developmental career services that incorporate contemporary developments in the field must be supported by evaluation of career services. This is the topic of Chapter 4.

Evaluating Career Services and Interventions

Evaluation of career development programs and interventions is important in an era of accountability (Sampson, Reardon, Peterson, & Lenz, 2004). As indicated by the competency framework for practitioners developed by the International Association for Educational and Vocational Guidance (IAEVG, 2003), it is also a professional responsibility. This chapter describes two approaches to evaluating career development programs and interventions. The first is a six-step sequential process for evaluating career counselling programs (Whiston & Brecheisen, 2002). The second is an accountability model from a cognitive information processing perspective (Sampson et al., 2004).

Six-Step Sequential Process for Evaluating Career Counselling

Step 1: Identifying the Focus of the Evaluation

The focus may be broad (e.g., a longitudinal evaluation of whole school career education program), or it may be more specific such as evaluating a short career workshop to teach students how to use online career and course exploration resources. Regardless of breadth, it is important to align the evaluation with the goals of the career intervention being evaluated (Whiston & Buck, 2008). In countries with national career development frameworks, the goals for career interventions may be constructed from selected career competencies and related performance indicators. This same selected set of competencies and performance indicators would be the focus of the evaluation study.

Consideration needs to be given as to whether formative evaluation, summative evaluation or both are required. For example, if the goal of a career development intervention were to improve career self-management skills, then both formative and summative evaluation may be desirable. Formative evaluation would identify gaps in career management skills. The relevant career competencies and related performance indicators would be the goals of a career intervention as well as defining a baseline against which changes in level of career management competence can be compared following a career intervention. Summative evaluation would determine the effectiveness of the intervention in improving career management competence.

Consideration needs to be given to the individuals or groups from which to gather data. In addition to a sample of recipients of a career intervention, there may be a range of other stakeholders who would provide useful information for the evaluation, such as teachers who delivered the program, parents or guardians, guests speakers, and external consultants who contributed to the program or intervention.

Step 2: Formulate the Evaluation Design and Procedures

Whenever possible, an evaluation study would be enhanced with data collection from a sample of recipients as well as a comparison group of students who did not participate in the career intervention. If the students who participated in the career intervention had significantly higher scores on an outcome measure than the comparison group, then there is greater certainty that the intervention was responsible for improved outcomes.

It can be difficult to use a comparison group in some school career intervention evaluation studies. For career interventions that are delivered to different classes or groups at different times, the wait-list procedure could be used. Using the wait-list procedure, the evaluation is conducted after the first group has completed the career intervention, but before the wait-list group participates in the career intervention. Differences between the students who participated in the intervention and the wait-list group should be the result of the intervention rather than some other factor. For career interventions that involve a whole year cohort on a particular day, such as a career expo or career conference, students in the same year cohort who were absent on that day may form a reasonable comparison group.

An evaluation study may be based on in-depth study of a small number of students who participated in the career intervention (Whiston & Buck, 2008). These authors note that there is a trend towards multimethod approaches to evaluations studies. Accordingly, in-depth case studies involving a small number of students may add depth to quantitative data collected from a larger sample of students.

Step 3: Determine the Evaluation Outcome Measures

The career management competencies and related performance indicators identified in career competency frameworks such as the Australian Blueprint for Career Development describe nationally standardised competencies that students can expect to gain as a result of participating in career interventions. Outcome measures can be designed to assess competence in the set of career competencies and performance indicators that are the focus of the career intervention being evaluated.

Depending on the goals of a career program or intervention, psychological instruments may be suitable to evaluate a career intervention. For example, if a goal of a career education intervention were to enhance career adaptability, the Career Adapt-Abilities Scale (Savickas & Porfeli, 2012) administered pre-test and post-might be a useful measure.

Step 4: Gather Program Information

Data collection needs to be planned in advance. In a school context this may involve negotiating with the school leadership team and other staff members to gain permission to use some class time for data gathering purposes. Pilot testing evaluation materials with a small group of students is a useful strategy to ensure that students understand the questions, the language used and the response procedure.

Step 5: Analyse and Interpret the Program Information

Depending on the nature of the evaluation methods and instrument, interpretation of results may be based on quantitative data, qualitative data or both. Mean, standard deviation and *t* test or other descriptive statistics may be sufficient for the quantitative data for some evaluation studies. Support from the school mathematics department may be helpful for career development facilitators who do not feel confident with inferential statistical analyses. Qualitative data avoids the need for statistical inference, although analysis and interpretation may be time consuming.

Step 6: Using the Information Gained

The final step is using the information gained from the evaluation study to make decisions about the career intervention. The information gained from the evaluation study may also be used to support requests for an increased share of the total school budget, improved staffing levels, improved physical resources, or at least maintaining existing levels. The results can be disseminated to stakeholder groups such as students, parents and guardians, alumni, business and community groups and shared with career development facilitators in other schools and school sectors.

The Cognitive Information Processing Approach to Accountability

The authors of the cognitive information processing career theory developed an accountability model to assess the effectiveness of career interventions (Sampson et al., 2004). There are two domains to this model: (1) effectiveness of services, and (2) cost to deliver services.

Effectiveness of Services

There are five components to this domain:

- **Component 1: Diagnosis.** This component refers to identifying student career development needs. The career development needs common to a group of students (e.g., a class or a year cohort) inform the goals of a career intervention. This step is similar to the formative evaluation approach described in the previous section.

- **Component 2: Prescription.** This component refers to the development of a learning program or plan to address diagnosed career development needs.

- **Component 3: Process.** This component involves documenting the processes and activities that will be undertaken so that students make progress towards the goals of the intervention.

- **Component 4: Outputs.** These outputs are primary student changes resulting from the career intervention. They refer to the new skills, knowledge and attitudes that students acquire directly as a result of the career intervention. This component includes identifying the outputs and the tools to assess them.

- **Component 5: Outcomes.** These outcomes refer to the secondary effects of a career intervention; that is, the consequences of students applying the new skills, knowledge, and attitudes gained as a result of the career interventions (Sampson et al., 2004, p. 270). In a school context, outcomes might include behaviours such as studying school subjects that are prerequisites for courses leading to preferred career options, applying for apprenticeships, completing a realistic and achievable yet flexible transition plan, preparing a résumé and cover letter that lands a job interview, winning a job following a successful interview, getting work experience in an occupation that is nontraditional for one's gender, applying for a university course, and so on. This final component involves assessing the outcomes of the career intervention.

An evaluation study might construct a suitable evaluation tool to measure outputs soon after the career intervention has been implemented and another instrument, such as a semistructured interview to explore the outcomes of the career intervention with a small group of students who participated in the intervention after an appropriate interval. In this way both the short- and longer-term effects of career interventions can be examined.

Cost to Deliver Services

The costs to deliver services domain assists schools to determine cost-effectiveness of career services or individual interventions. Sampson et al. (2004) suggest that the cost of running a career development intervention can be approximated by itemising and summing costs for the components of staff (professional and administrative), expenses such as materials and supplies required to develop and deliver career interventions, capital equipment (e.g., computers, furniture, shelving, etc.) and overhead costs (electricity, rent, water, etc.). A ratio of output to cost can be calculated as one indicator of cost-effectiveness. In a school context it may be impractical to include overhead costs and potentially also capital costs when calculating the cost of career interventions. Nevertheless, the notion of calculating the cost of individual career interventions and indeed a whole career development program over a school year is an important one, particularly in an age of accountability and restricted resources (Sampson et al., 2004).

Chapter 5

Concluding Comments

School career services should address the career development needs of students. They need to provide answers to
career questions that students typically ask. These questions
are mostly concerned with the career issues that students are
currently facing, or will face in the near future, such as
choosing school subjects, getting a part-time or holiday job,
or applying for post-school courses. However, schools need to
prepare students for the longer term. School career services
must prepare students to be able to self-manage their career in
an unpredictable and changing future world of work. An
understanding of theories relevant to the career development
of school students can help career development facilitators to
feel confident about their capacity to meet the current career
development needs of students and to foster the development
of lifelong career management skills.

Career development theory and research informs us that
school career services should take a developmental perspective. Career interventions should be consistent with students'
stage of career development and the vocational development
tasks they are facing. In the upper middle and secondary years
this is likely to begin with career interventions that orient
students to the importance of the work role and the vocational development tasks they will confront. Career
interventions that facilitate students' capacity to explore
possible selves and future learning and work scenarios, learn
about the world of work and develop career decision-making
skills and the confidence to successfully implement career

preferences are important aspects of school career services for students in the upper middle and secondary years. These competencies will equip students to manage their career throughout life.

Career development theories provide the content of career development services and guide career development facilitators in ways of working with students in relation to their career development. For career development facilitators who do not feel sufficiently comfortable with the content of career theories, the national career development frameworks of lifelong career management competencies are useful resources for designing and implementing developmentally appropriate career services in schools.

Career intervention research has provided guidelines on the components of quality career services. Ideally, career programs should incorporate as many of the five critical ingredients of effective career interventions as possible (Brown & Ryan Krane, 2000; Brown et al., 2003). The cognitive information processing approach to differentiated service delivery enables the benefits of life design counselling on an individual basis to be offered to those who need it most and group or self-help intervention modalities for other students. However, some life designing tools such as My System of Career Influences (McMahon, Patton, & Watson, 2005) or My Career Story (Savickas & Hartung, 2012) may also be useful in other career intervention modalities such as workshops or small group career counselling.

On a final note, accountability, continuous improvement and continued support from the school administration and wider community are important reasons for regular evaluation of school career services.

References

Athanasou, J.A. (2000). *A brief, free and standardized assessment of interests for use in educational and vocational guidance (Version 3.1)*. Sydney, Australia: University of Technology.

Athanasou, J.A. (2007). *Manual for the Career Interest Test (Version 4.1)*. Sydney, Australia: University of Technology.

Bartlett, C., Perera, H. N., & McIlveen, P. (2015). A short form of the Career Interest Test: 21-CIT. *Journal of Career Assessment*, 1–13.

Blustein, D.L. (2006). *The psychology of working: A new perspective for career development, counseling, and public policy*. Mahwah, NJ: Lawrence Earlbaum.

Bride, M. (1995). *A comparison of the levels of students' career maturity resulting from two models for the delivery of career education programs in selected Victorian government secondary schools* (Unpublished master's thesis). Deakin University, Melbourne, Australia.

Bright, J.E.H. & Pryor, R.G.L. (2007). Chaotic careers assessment: How constructivist perspectives and psychometric techniques can be integrated into work and life decision making. *Career Planning and Adult Development Journal*, *23*, 30–48.

Bright, J.E.H & Pryor, R.G.L. (2008). Shiftwork: A chaos theory of careers agenda for change in career counselling. *Australian Journal of Career Development*, *17*, 63–72.

Brott, P.E. (2001). The storied approach: A post-modern approach for career counseling. *The Career Development Quarterly*, *49*, 304–312.

Brown, S.D., & Ryan Krane, N.E. (2000). Four (or five) sessions and a cloud of dust: Old assumptions and new observations about career counseling. In S.D. Brown, & R.W. Lent (Eds.), *Handbook of counseling psychology* (3rd ed., pp. 740–766). New York, NY: Wiley.

Brown, S.D., Ryan Krane, N.E., Brecheisen, J., Castelino, P., Budisin, I., Miller, M., & Edens, L. (2003). Critical ingredients of career choice interventions: More analyses and new hypotheses. *Journal of Vocational Behavior, 62*, 411–428.

Education Services Australia. (2015). Projects. myfuture. Retrieved from http://www.myfuture.edu.au

Gollert, K. (2003). *Developing a career information centre* (5th ed.). Retrieved from http://ccia-acadop.ca/wp-content/uploads/2011/07/Developing-a-Career-Information-Centre.pdf

Gottfredson, L.S. (1981). Circumscription and compromise: A developmental theory of occupational aspirations [Monograph]. *Journal of Counseling Psychology, 28*, 545–579.

Gottfredson, L.S. (1996). Gottfredson's theory of circumscription and compromise. In D. Brown & L. Brooks (Eds.), *Career choice and development* (2nd ed., pp. 179–232). San Francisco, CA: Jossey-Bass.

Gottfredson, L.S. (2002). Gottfredson's theory of circumscription, compromise, and self-creation. In D. Brown (Ed.), *Career choice and development* (4th ed., pp. 85–148). San Francisco, CA: Jossey-Bass.

Gottfredson, L.S. (2005). Applying Gottfredson's theory of circumscription and compromise in career guidance and counseling. In S.D. Brown & R.W. Lent (Eds.), *Career development and counseling: Putting theory and research to work* (pp. 71–100). Hoboken, NJ: Wiley.

Hartung, P.J. (2013a). Career as story: Making the narrative turn. In B. Walsh, M.L. Savickas, M.L., & P.J. Hartung, (Eds.), *Handbook of vocational psychology: Theory, research, and practice* (4th ed., pp. 33–52). New York, NY: Routledge.

Hartung, P.J. (2013b). The life-span, life-space theory of careers. In S.D. Brown & R.W. Lent (Eds.), *Career development and counseling: Putting theory and research to work* (2nd ed., pp. 83–113). Hoboken, NJ: Wiley.

Hartung, P.J. (2015). The career construction interview. In M. McMahon & M. Watson (Eds.), *Career assessment: Qualitative approaches* (pp. 115–121). Rotterdam, the Netherlands: Sense.

Holland, J.L. (1959). A theory of vocational choice. *Journal of Counseling Psychology, 6,* 35–45.

Holland, J.L. (1997). *Making vocational choices: A theory of vocational personalities and work environments* (3rd ed.). Odessa, FL: Psychological Assessment Resources.

Hughes, C., & Lenz, J.G. (2011). A cognitive information processing (CIP) approach to career services: An Australian case study. *Australian Career Practitioner, 22,* 11–13.

International Association for Educational and Vocational Guidance. (IAEVG). (2003). *International competencies for educational and vocational guidance practitioners.* Retrieved from http://iaevg.net/iaevg.org/IAEVG/index00a8.html?lang=2

Loader, T. (2009). Careers Collage: Applying an art therapy technique to career development in a secondary school setting. *Australian Career Practitioner, 20,* 16–17.

Lokan, J. (1992). The Work Importance Study: Australian young people's values in international perspective. In M. Poole (Ed.), *Education and Work* (pp. 180–211).

Hawthorn, Australia: Australian Council of Educational Research.

Lokan, J.J. & Shears, M. (1995). Studies of work importance in Australia. In D.E. Super & B. Sverko (Eds.), *Life roles, values, and careers: International findings of the Work Importance Study* (pp. 77–99). San Francisco, CA: Jossey-Bass.

McIlveen, P. (2006). *My career chapter: A dialogical autobiography.* Unpublished manuscript.

McIlveen, P., Ford, T., & Dun, K. (2005). A narrative sentence-completion process for systems career assessment. *Australian Journal of Career Development, 14,* 30–39.

Ministerial Council for Education, Early Childhood Development and Youth Affairs (MCEECDYA). (2010). *The Australian blueprint for career development,* prepared by Miles Morgan Australia, Commonwealth of Australia, Canberra. Available at http://education.gov.au/australian-blueprint-career-development

McMahon, M., Patton, W., & Watson, M. (2005). *My system of career influences (MSCI): Facilitator's buide.* Camberwell, Australia: ACER Press.

McMahon, M. & Watson, M. (2012). Telling stories of career assessment. *Journal of Career Assessment, 20,* 440–451.

McMahon, M. & Watson, M. (2015). (Eds.). *Career assessment: Qualitative approaches* (pp. 115–121). Rotterdam, the Netherlands: Sense.

Patton, W. & Creed, P.A. (2002). The relationship between career maturity and work commitment in a sample of Australian high school students. *Journal of Career Development, 29,* 69–85.

Patton, W. & McMahon, M. (1999). *Career development and systems theory: A new relationship.* Pacific Grove, CA: Brooks/Cole.

Patton, W. & McMahon, M. (2006). *Career development and systems theory: Connecting theory and practice* (2nd ed.). Rotterdam, the Netherlands: Sense.

Patton, W. & McMahon, M. (2014). *Career development and systems theory: Connecting theory and practice* (3rd ed.). Rotterdam, the Netherlands: Sense.

Pepper, S.C. (1942). *World hypotheses: A study in evidence.* Berkeley: University of California Press.

Peterson, G.W., Sampson, J.P., Jr., Lenz, J.G., & Reardon, R.C. (2002). A cognitive information processing approach to career problem solving and decision making. In D. Brown (Ed.), *Career choice and development* (4th ed., pp. 312–369). San Francisco, CA: Jossey-Bass.

Pryor, R.G.L., Amundson, N.E., & Bright, J.E.H. (2008). Probabilities and possibilities: The strategic counseling implications of the chaos theory of careers. *The Career Development Quarterly,* 56, 309-318.

Pryor, R.G.L., Bright, J.E.H. (2003). The chaos theory of careers. *Australian Journal of Career Development,* *12,* 12–20.

Pryor, R. & Bright, J. (2011). *The chaos theory of careers: A new perspective on working in the twenty-first century.* New York, NY: Routledge.

Pryor, R.G.L. & Bright, J.E.H. (2015). Chaotic career assessment: Integrating quantitative and qualitative career assessment. In M. McMahon & M. Watson (Eds.), *Career assessment: Qualitative approaches* (pp. 191–198). Rotterdam, the Netherlands: Sense.

Richardson, M.S. (1993). Work in people's lives: A location for counseling psychologists. *Journal of Counseling Psychology,* *40,* 425–433.

Richardson, M.S., Constantine, K., & Washburn, M. (2005). New directions for theory development in vocational psychology. In W.B. Walsh & M.L. Savickas (Eds.), *Handbook of vocational psychology* (3rd ed., pp. 51–83). Mahwah, NJ: Lawrence Erlbaum.

Rounds, J., Walker, C.M., Day, S.X., Hubert, S.L., Lewis, P, & Rivkin, D., (1999). *O*Net™ interest profiler: Reliability, validity, and self-scoring* [Online]. Retrieved from https://www.onetcenter.org/dl_files/IP_RVS.pdf

Sampson, J.P., Jr. (2009). Modern and postmodern career theories: The unnecessary divorce. *The Career Development Quarterly, 58*, 91–96.

Sampson, J.P., Jr., Lenz, J.G., Reardon, R.C., & Peterson, G.W. (1999). A cognitive information processing approach to employment problem solving and decision making. *The Career Development Quarterly, 48*, 3–18.

Sampson, J.P., Peterson, G.W., Lenz, J.G., & Reardon, R.C. (1992). A cognitive approach to career development and services: Translating concepts into practice. *The Career Development Quarterly, 41*, 67–74.

Sampson, J.P., Peterson, G.W., Lenz, J.G., Reardon, R.C., & Saunders, D.E. (1996). *Career Thoughts Inventory*. Odessa, FL: Psychological Assessment Resources.

Sampson, J.P., Reardon, R.C., Peterson, G.W. & Lenz, J.G. (2004). *Career counseling & services: A cognitive information processing approach*. Belmont, CA: Brooks/Cole – Thompson Learning.

Savickas, M.L. (1993). Career counseling in the postmodern era. *Journal of Cognitive Psychotherapy: An International Quarterly, 7*, 205–215.

Savickas, M.L. (2002). Career construction theory. In D. Brown (Ed.). *Career choice and development* (4th ed., pp. 149–205). San Francisco, CA: Jossey-Bass.

Savickas, M.L. (2005). The theory and practice of career construction. In S.D. Brown & R.W. Lent (Eds.), *Career development and counseling: Putting theory and research to work* (pp. 42-70). Hokoben, NJ: Wiley.

Savickas, M.L. (2011). New questions for vocational psychology: Premises, paradigms, and practices. *Journal of Career Assessment, 19*, 251-258.

Savickas, M.L. (2012). A paradigm for career intervention in the 21st Century. *Journal of Counseling and Development, 90*, 13–19.

Savickas, M.L. (2013a). Constructing careers: Actors, agents, and authors. *The Counseling Psychologist, 41*, 648–662.

Savickas, M.L. (2013b). Career construction theory and practice. In S.D. Brown & R.W. Lent, *Career development and counseling: Putting theory and research to work* (2nd ed., pp. 147–183). Hoboken, NJ: Wiley.

Savickas, M.L. (2015). *The life-design counselling manual.* Retrieved from http://www.vocopher.com/LifeDesign/LifeDesign.pdf

Savickas, M.L. & Baker, D.B. (2005). The history of vocational psychology: Antecedents, origin, and early development. In W.B. Walsh & M.L. Savickas. *Handbook of vocational psychology* (3rd ed., pp. 15–50). Mahwah, NJ: Lawrence Erlbaum.

Savickas, M.L., & Hartung, P.J. (2012). *My career story: An autiobiographical workbook for life-career success.* Retrieved from http://www.vocopher.com/CSI/CCI_workbook.pdf

Savickas, M.L., Nota, L., Rossier J., Dauwaldr J.-P., Duart, M.E., Guichard, J., Soresi, S., Van Esbroeck, R., & van Vianen, A.E.M. (2009). Life designing: A paradigm for career construction in the 21st century. *Journal of Vocational Behavior, 75*, 239–250.

Savickas, M.L. & Porfeli, E.J. (2012). Career Adapt-Abilities Scale: Construction, reliability, and measurement equivalence across 13 countries. *Journal of Vocational Behavior, 80*, 661–673.

Super, D.E. (1953). A theory of vocational development. *The American Psychologist, 8*, 185–190.

Super, D.E. (1980). A life-span, life-space approach to career development. *Journal of Vocational Behavior, 16*, 282–298.

Super, D.E. (1983). Assessment in career guidance: Toward truly developmental counseling. *The Personnel and Guidance Journal, 61*, 555–562.

Super, D.E. (1990). A life-span, life-space approach to career development. In D. Brown and L. Brooks (Eds.), *Career choice and development: Applying contemporary theories to practice* (2nd ed., pp. 197–261). San Francisco, CA: Jossey-Bass.

Super, D.E., Savickas, M.L., & Super, C.M. (1996). The life-span, life-space approach to careers. In D. Brown, & L. Brooks (Eds.), *Career choice and development* (3rd ed., pp. 121–178). San Francisco, CA: Jossey-Bass.

US Department of Labor (2015). O*Net Interest Profiler. Retrieved from http://www.mynextmove.org/explore/ip

Vondracek, F.W., Ford, D.H., Porfeli, E.J. (2014). *A living systems theory of vocational behavior and development.* Rotterdam, the Netherlands: Sense.

Watson, M., & McMahon, M. (2014). Making meaning of quantitative assessment in career counseling through a storytelling approach. In G. Arulmani, A. Bakshi, F. Leong, & T. Watts (Eds.), *Handbook of career development: International perspectives* (pp. 631–644). New York, NY: Springer.

Whiston, S.C. (2002). Application of the principles: Career counseling and interventions. *The Counseling Psychologist, 30*, 218–237.

Whiston, S.C., & Brecheisen, B. (2002). Evaluating the effectiveness of adult career development programs. In S.G. Niles (Ed.), *Adult career development: Concepts, issues, and practices* (3rd ed., pp. 367–384). Alexandria, VA: National Career Development Association.

Whiston, S.C. & Buck, I.M. (2008). Evaluation of career guidance programs. In J. Athanasou & R. van Estbroeck. *International handbook of career guidance* (pp. 677–692). Dordrecht, the Netherlands: Springer-Science.

Whiston, S.C., Sexton, T.L., & Lasoff, D.L. (1998). Career-intervention outcome: A replication and extension of Oliver and Spokane (1988). *Journal of Counseling Psychology, 45*, 150–165.

Young, R.A., Valach, L., & Collin, A. (2002). A contextualist explanation of career. In D. Brown (Ed.), *Career choice and development* (4th ed., pp. 207–251). San Francisco, CA: Jossey-Bass.